St. Patrick's Day
Activity Book for Kids

Mazes, Coloring and Puzzles for Kids 4 – 8

Young Scholar

All rights reserved. No part of this document may be reproduced Used or transmitted in any form or by any means, electronic or otherwise. This means you cannot photocopy any material ideas or tips that are provided in this book.

Young Scholar
Published by Ciparum LLC

St. Patrick's Day Activity Book for Kids
© 2017 Young Scholar
All rights reserved.
ISBN-10:1-63589-302-X
ISBN-13:978-1-63589-302-1

www.youngscholar.co

Other Books in this Series

Christmas Day Activity Book for Kids
Valentine's Day Activity Book for Kids
Halloween Activity Book for Kids
Thanksgiving Day Activity Book for Kids

For more engaging activity books, visit:

www.youngscholar.co

ST. PATRICK'S DAY

_____
_____
_____
_____

17 MARCH

Match the shadow to the right Leprechaun

Help the Leprechaun get the gold

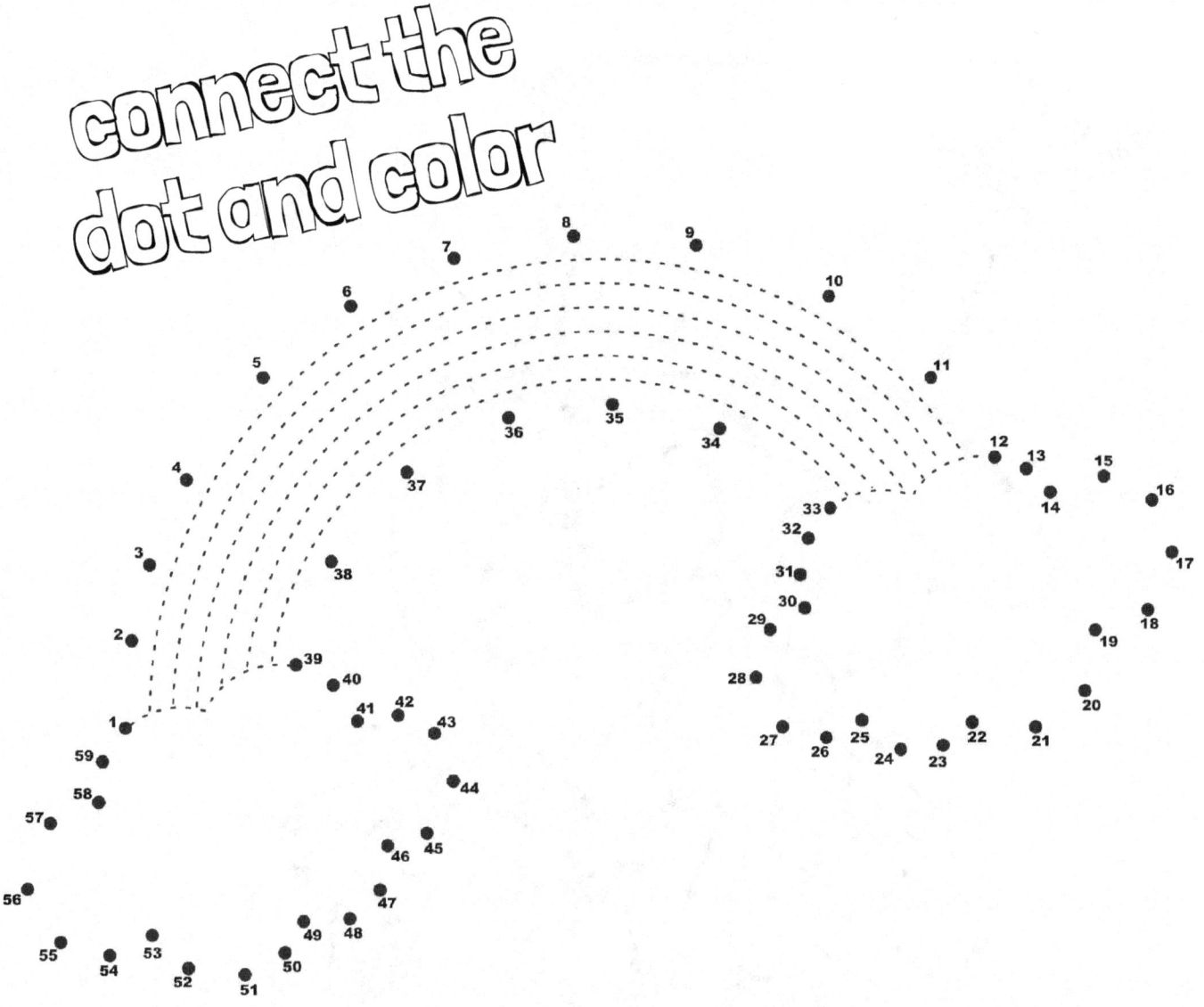

HOW MANY

LEPRECHAUNS

DO YOU SEE?

connect each kid to a pot of gold

LINK THE IMAGE TO ITS SHADOW

COLOR ME!

Find the correct shadow

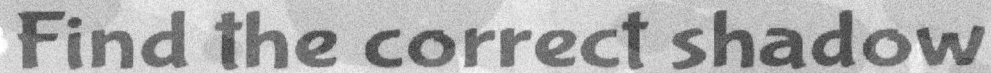

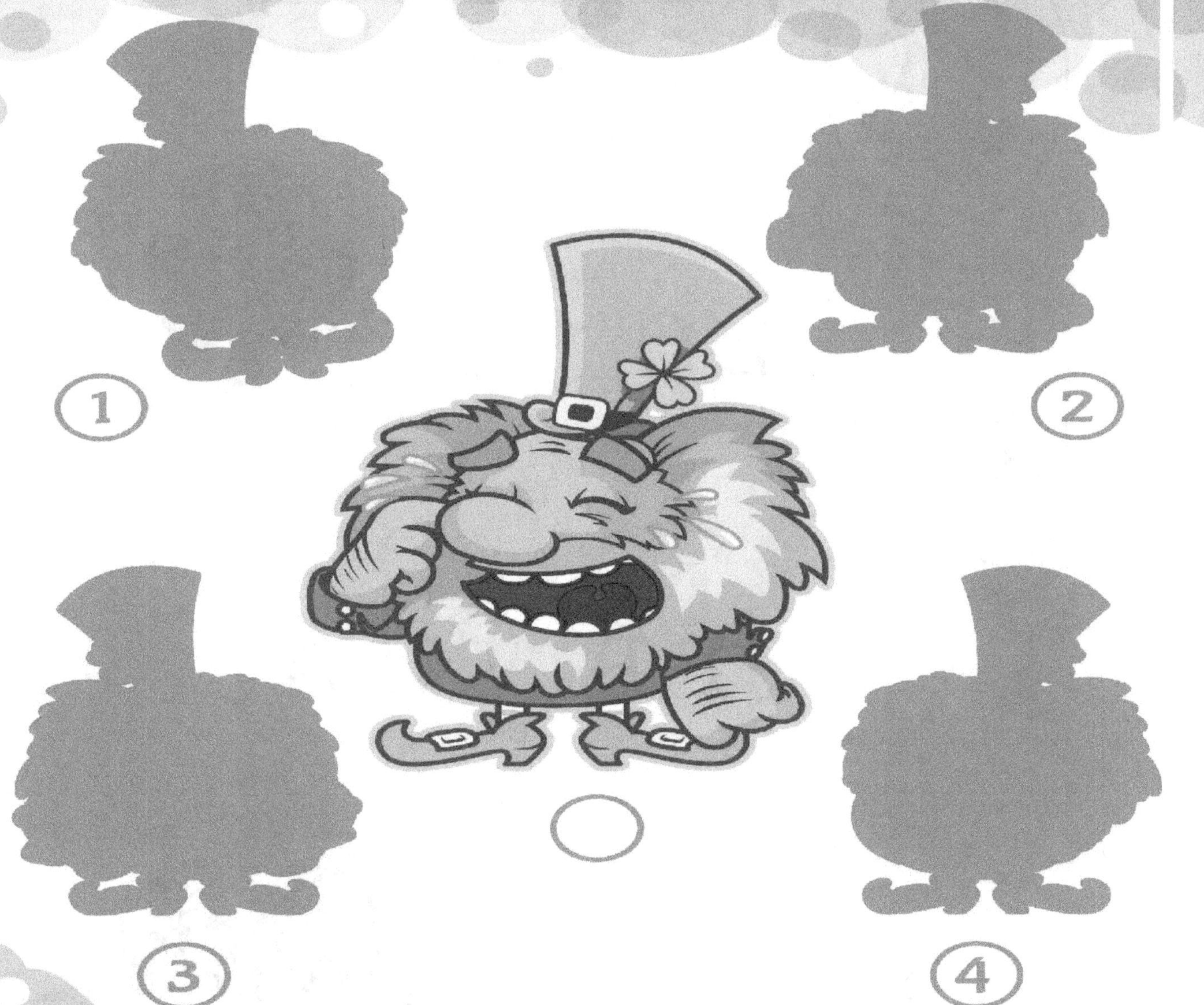

Fill in the missing letters

_ L O _ _ R

_ _ P R _ _ H A _ _

_ _ L _ _ _ T

Help Little Let get to some pizza slice!

Find the clover book

dot to dot

Connect the dots and color

Complete and Color

Help Lep get to his friends

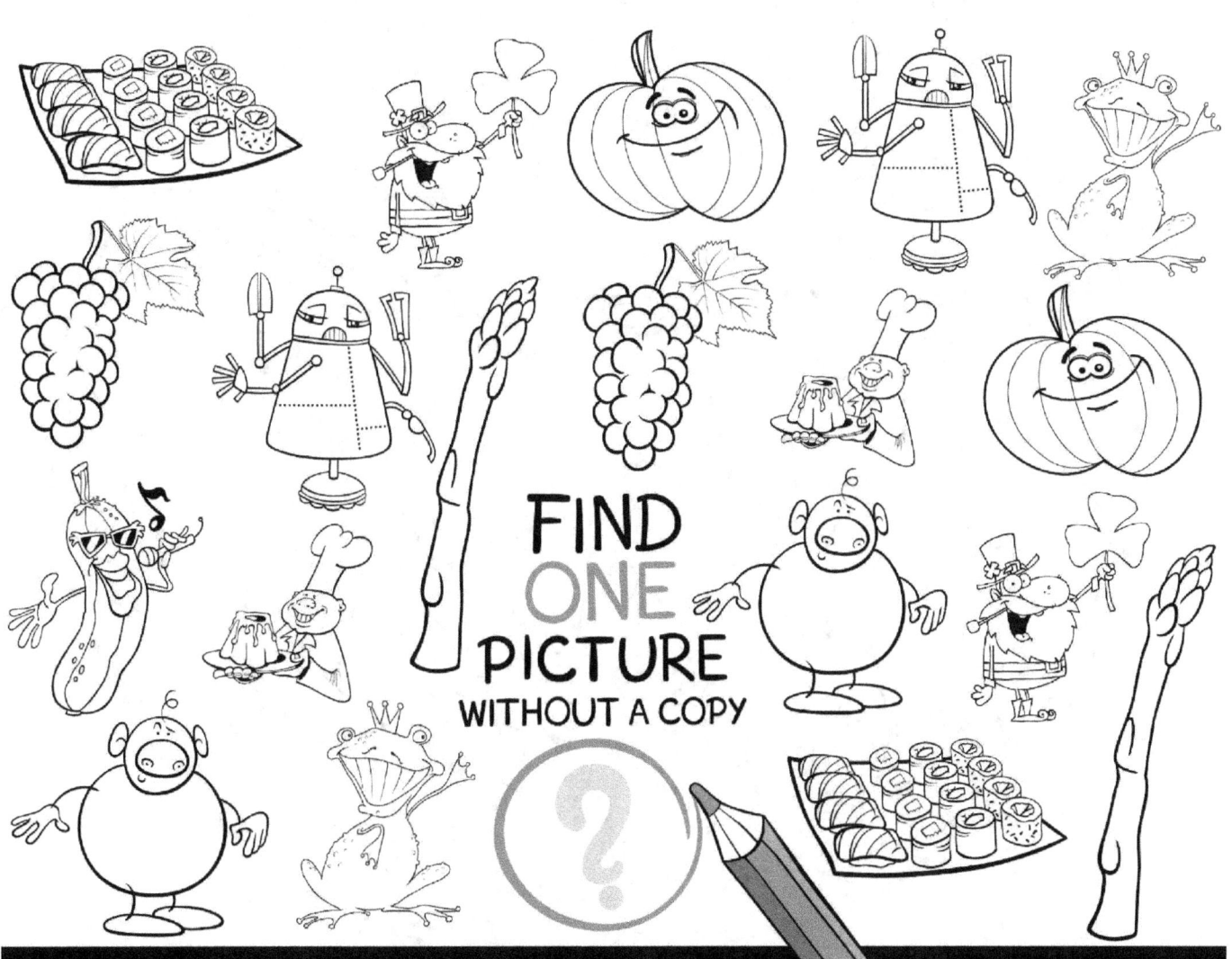

Guide to clover pot

Color me

Guide the Leprechaun to the gold

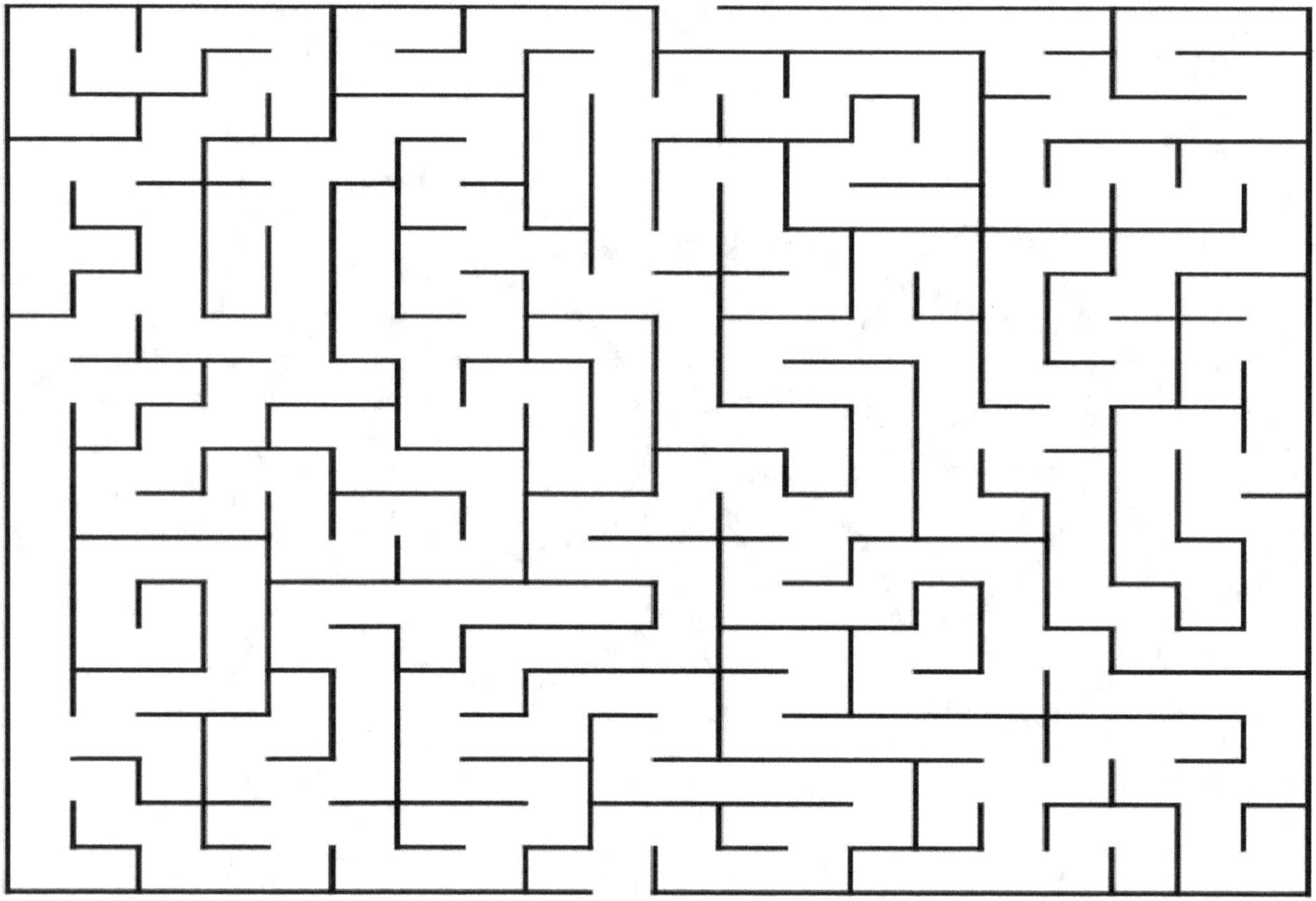

Get the gold

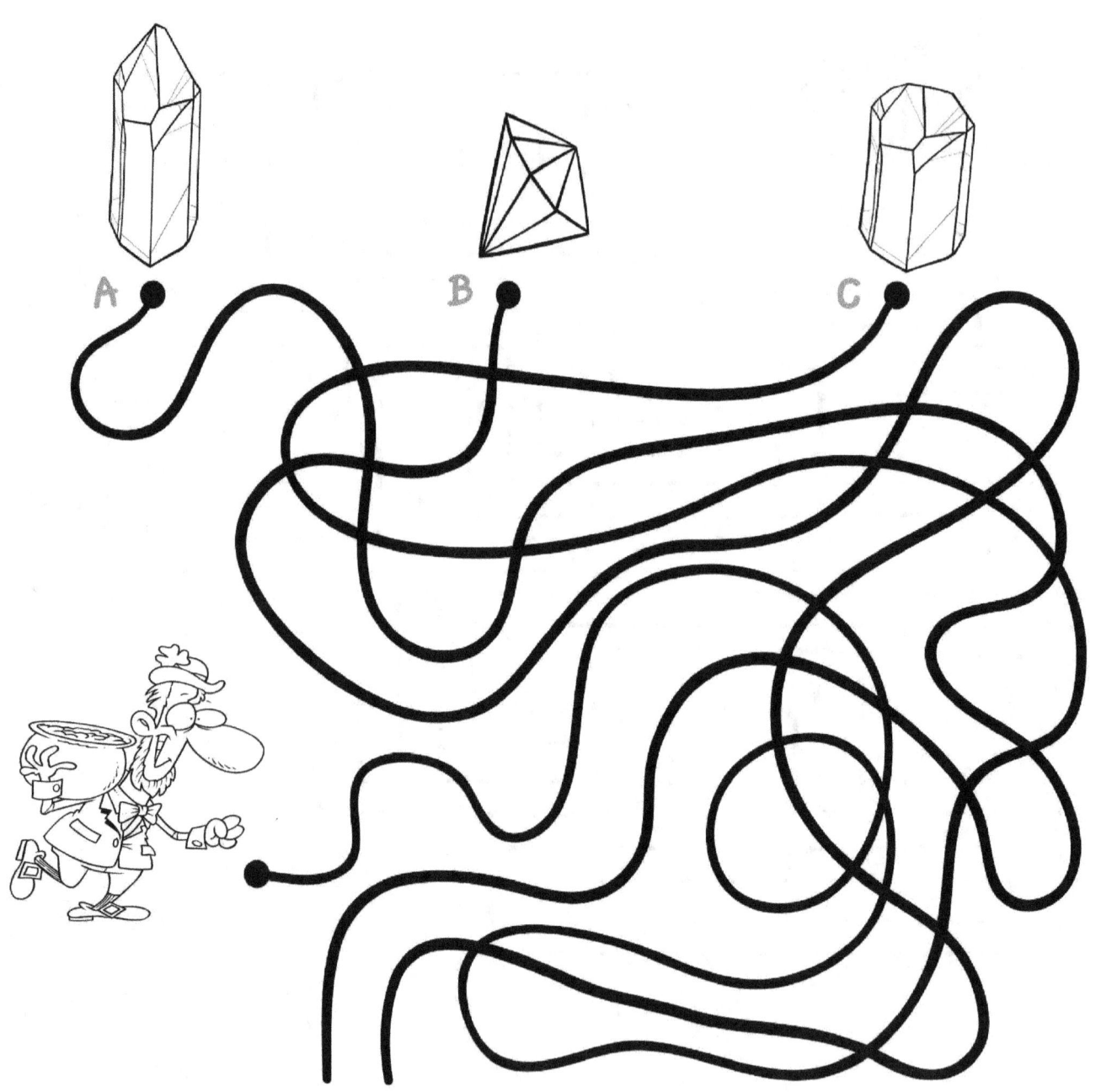

Help Junior get to his dad

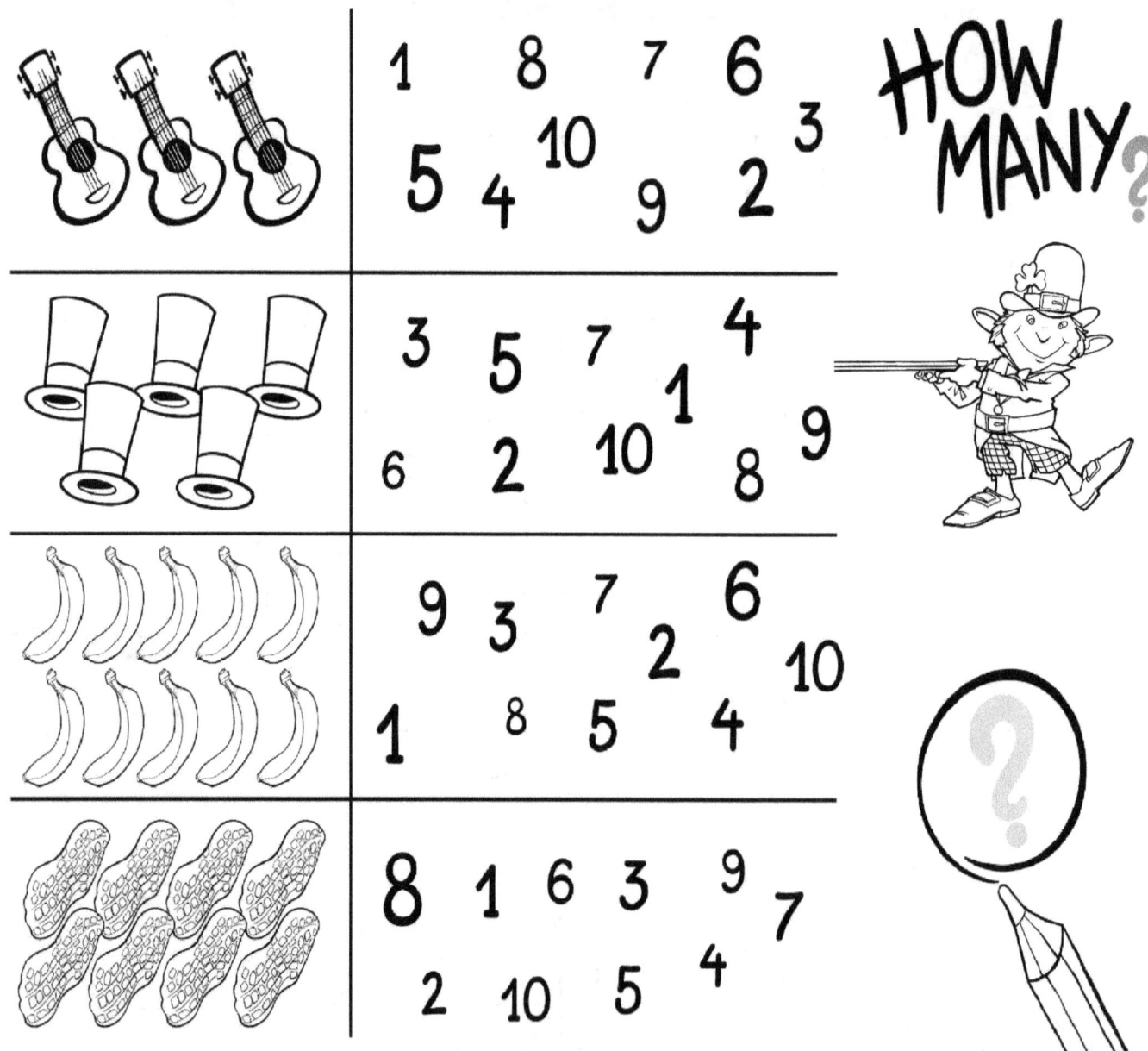

What do you see?
Fill in the missing alphabets

_ E _ R _ C _ A _ N

R _ I _ _ O _

_ L _ _ E _

Who gets the diamond?

Lead the way to Gold!

Write the correct alphabet in the square

R - 2   B - 1
I - 6   N - 7
A - 5
W - 4
O - 3

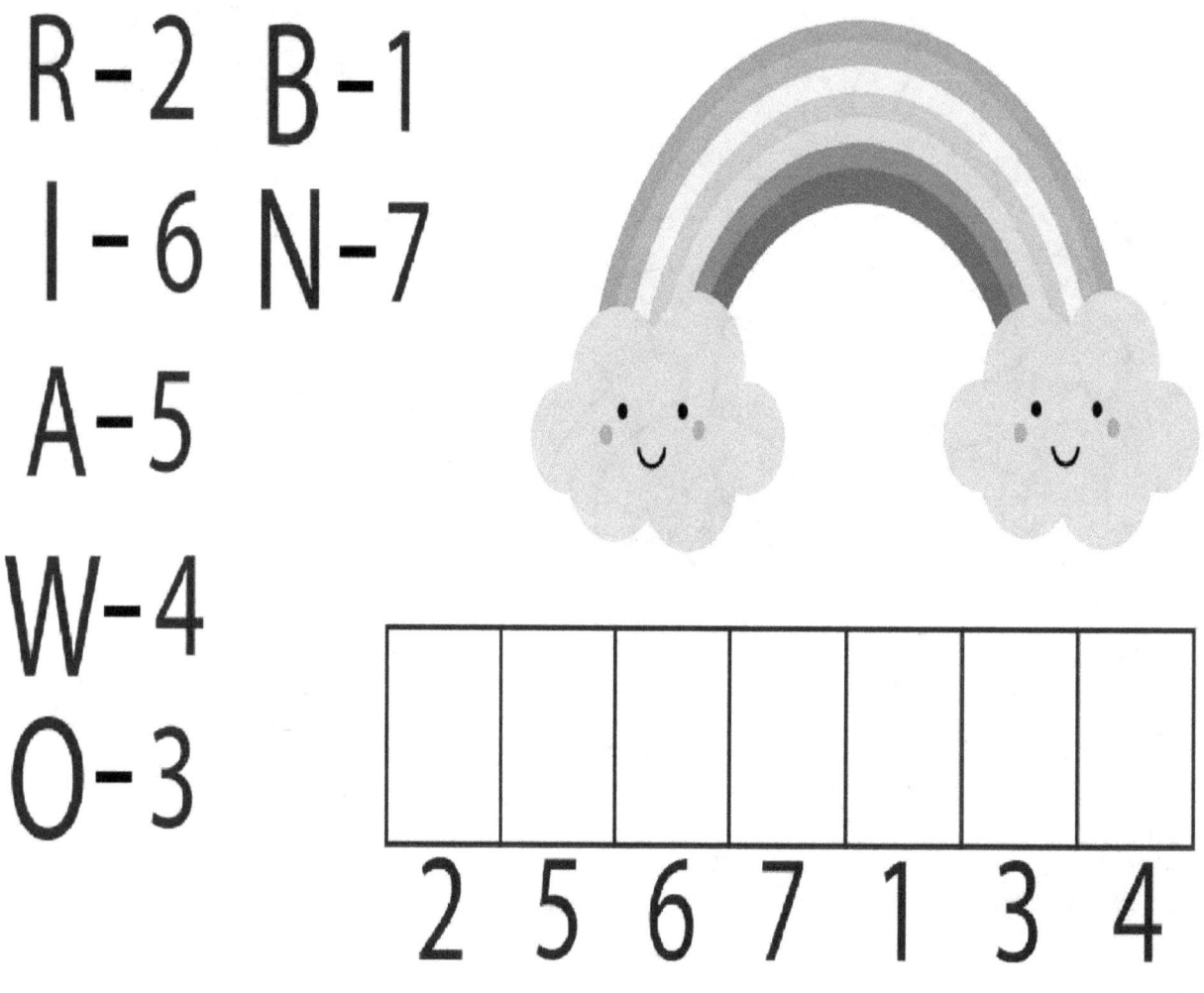

2	5	6	7	1	3	4

Guide to gold

Awesome!

www.ingramcontent.com/pod-product-compliance
Lightning Source LLC
Chambersburg PA
CBHW051424070526
44584CB00023B/3571